Balanced Mind, Balanced Life

A Guide to Mental Health Practices

Aria Vitality

DEDICATION

To all those who strive for inner peace, balance, and well-being amidst life's myriad challenges. Your courage, resilience, and commitment to personal growth inspire the pages of this book. May these words serve as a guiding light on your journey towards a harmonious and fulfilled life.

CONTENTS

ACKNOWLEDGMENTS

This book is the culmination of collective wisdom, support, and encouragement from numerous individuals and resources. I extend my deepest gratitude to all those who have contributed to its creation.

To my family and friends, thank you for your unwavering love, patience, and understanding throughout this endeavor. Your support has been my anchor during moments of doubt and inspiration during times of creativity.

I am indebted to the mental health professionals whose expertise and dedication have shaped the content of this book. Your commitment to helping others navigate the complexities of the mind is truly commendable.

To the readers who embark on this journey of self-discovery and growth, thank you for entrusting me with your time and attention. It is my sincere hope that the insights shared within these pages resonate with you and empower you to cultivate a life of balance, resilience, and fulfillment.

Finally, I extend my heartfelt appreciation to the team at SmartWave Research Group, whose professionalism, guidance, and enthusiasm have brought this project to fruition.

With deep appreciation,
Aria Vitality

The Path to Inner Harmony

Have you ever felt like you're running on a treadmill, constantly striving but never quite reaching a sense of peace and fulfillment? Perhaps you juggle a demanding career, navigate complex relationships, and wrestle with a nagging voice in your head that whispers doubts. This was certainly my experience for a long time. I chased external validation, equated productivity with self-worth, and neglected the crucial foundation of my mental well-being. It wasn't until I embarked on a journey of self-discovery that I began to understand the power of prioritizing my mental health.

This journey wasn't linear or easy. There were stumbles and setbacks, moments of overwhelming stress, and days when negative thoughts felt like a constant barrage. But with each step, I learned valuable tools and practices that helped me cultivate inner harmony. This book is an invitation to join me on a similar exploration.

Here, we'll delve into the importance of holistic mental health practices. We'll move beyond simply managing stress and delve into building a life that fosters genuine well-being. We'll explore how self-awareness, healthy habits, and strong relationships can serve as the cornerstones of a balanced life. We'll tackle the inner critic, navigate challenges with a growth mindset, and discover the importance of prioritizing fun and play. Most importantly, we'll explore the power of seeking professional support when needed.

This book is not a collection of quick fixes, but rather a roadmap to sustainable mental well-being. Think of it as a toolbox filled with practical strategies and techniques that you can personalize for your unique journey. Through self-reflection, exploration, and consistent effort, you can cultivate a sense of inner peace and build a life that feels authentically fulfilling. So, take a deep breath, turn the page, and let's embark on this path to inner harmony together.

CHAPTER 1

THE FOUNDATION - BUILDING SELF-AWARENESS

The Cornerstone of Well-being

Imagine yourself standing at the base of a magnificent building. Towering above you, it represents your overall well-being. But before you can begin constructing the sturdy walls and expansive rooms of this metaphorical structure, you need a strong foundation – a foundation built on self-awareness.

Mental health is not simply the absence of mental illness. It's a dynamic state of well-being that impacts how we think, feel, and act. It shapes how we manage stress, relate to others, and make choices. Just as a strong foundation ensures a building's stability, strong self-awareness is the bedrock on which a balanced and fulfilling life is built.

The Butterfly Effect of Mental Health

Think of your mental health as a butterfly. A small change in its environment, a gentle breeze perhaps, can have a ripple effect, influencing the trajectory of its flight. Similarly, our mental well-being impacts every aspect of our daily lives.

Feeling stressed or anxious? Productivity plummets, and relationships become strained. Experiencing low self-esteem? Our motivation wanes, and opportunities might slip through our fingers. Conversely, strong mental health empowers us to navigate challenges with resilience, fosters healthy connections with others, and fuels our pursuit of happiness.

Knowing Yourself: A Map to Your Emotions

Building self-awareness begins with understanding your emotions. We all experience a spectrum of emotions – joy, sadness, anger, fear, and everything in between. Yet, sometimes it can feel like these emotions control us rather than the other way around.

The first step to emotional awareness is acknowledging what you're feeling. Pay attention to your body's signals. A racing heart might indicate anxiety, while a clenched jaw could be a sign of frustration. Notice how your emotions manifest in your thoughts and behaviors. Are you prone to isolating yourself when feeling sad? Do you become overly critical of yourself when stressed?

Unearthing the Triggers: Why We Feel the Way We Do

Emotions rarely appear in isolation. Often, they're triggered by specific events, thoughts, or situations. Identifying these triggers is a crucial step in understanding and managing your emotions. For example, perhaps public speaking triggers feelings of anxiety. Maybe deadlines at work spark a sense of overwhelm. Once you recognize the triggers, you can develop effective coping mechanisms to navigate them with more ease.

Self-Compassion: The Antidote to Harsh Self-Criticism

Our journey to self-awareness isn't always sunshine and rainbows. There will be times when you stumble, make mistakes, or experience negative emotions. But here's the key: self-compassion is not the same as self-pity. It's about treating yourself with the same kindness and understanding you would offer a close friend.

Instead of berating yourself for a lapse in judgment, acknowledge that everyone makes mistakes. Instead of dwelling on negative thoughts, practice self-forgiveness and focus on learning from the experience.

Building self-awareness is an ongoing process. It requires dedication, patience, and a willingness to explore the depths of your own being. But with each step you take on this journey, you'll gain a deeper understanding of yourself and build a foundation for a truly balanced and fulfilling life.

CHAPTER 2

THE POWER OF HEALTHY HABITS

Building Blocks for a Balanced Life

The foundation of self-awareness is crucial, but it's only the first step. Just as a strong foundation needs supportive walls, our mental well-being thrives when nurtured by healthy habits. These habits become the building blocks of a balanced life, promoting mental clarity, emotional stability, and overall well-being.

The Symphony of Sleep: Rest for Body and Mind

Imagine your brain as a complex orchestra. During sleep, the musicians – your neurons – get a chance to rest and recharge. When sleep-deprived, this orchestra becomes discordant, leading to difficulty concentrating, emotional dysregulation, and increased vulnerability to stress.

Prioritizing sleep hygiene is essential for mental well-being.

Establish a consistent sleep schedule, even on weekends. Create a relaxing bedtime routine that might include taking a warm bath, reading a book, or practicing gentle stretches. Optimize your sleep environment by ensuring your bedroom is dark, quiet, and cool.

Fueling Your Well-being: The Art of Balanced Eating

Just as a car needs high-quality fuel to run smoothly, our bodies and minds rely on nutritious food to function optimally. A balanced diet rich in fruits, vegetables, whole grains, and lean protein provides the essential vitamins, minerals, and antioxidants that support mental well-being.

On the other hand, processed foods high in sugar and unhealthy fats can contribute to mood swings, fatigue, and difficulty concentrating. Focus on mindful eating, savoring each bite and paying attention to your body's hunger cues. Don't skip meals, as this can lead to energy crashes and unhealthy food choices later.

Move Your Body, Boost Your Mood

Physical exercise isn't just about physical fitness; it's a powerful tool for promoting mental well-being. Exercise releases endorphins, natural mood-lifters that combat stress and anxiety. It also improves sleep quality, increases energy levels, and boosts self-esteem.

Find an activity you enjoy, whether it's brisk walking, dancing, swimming, or team sports. Start slowly and gradually increase the intensity and duration of your workouts. Even small bursts of movement throughout the day can make a significant difference.

Finding Your Calm: Relaxation Techniques for a Stressed World

Modern life is full of stressors. Left unchecked, chronic stress can take a toll on our mental and physical health. Fortunately, there are a variety of relaxation techniques that can help us combat stress and cultivate a sense of inner peace.

Deep breathing exercises are a simple yet effective way to activate the body's relaxation response. Meditation helps quiet the mind and cultivate a sense of present-moment awareness. Progressive muscle relaxation involves tensing and releasing different muscle groups, promoting physical and mental relaxation.

Explore different techniques and find what works best for you. Dedicate a few minutes each day to practicing relaxation techniques, and you'll be surprised at how much calmer and more centered you feel.

Building healthy habits takes time and commitment. Don't be discouraged by occasional setbacks. Celebrate your progress, no matter how small, and remember that consistency is key. By incorporating these practices into your daily routine, you'll be well on your way to fostering a sense of well-being that empowers you to navigate life's challenges with greater resilience.

CHAPTER 3

Cultivating Mindfulness: Anchoring Yourself in the Present

Imagine yourself rushing through life on autopilot, constantly dwelling on the past or worrying about the future. Mindfulness offers an antidote to this autopilot mode, inviting us to be fully present in the here and now. By cultivating mindfulness, we can savor the simple joys of life, manage stress more effectively, and experience a greater sense of calm and clarity.

The Present Moment: A Sanctuary from the Storm

Our minds are often preoccupied with the "what ifs" of the future or replaying events of the past. Mindfulness encourages us to gently refocus our attention on the present moment. This isn't about emptying your mind or achieving a state of perfect zen. It's simply about becoming aware of your thoughts, feelings, and bodily sensations without judgment.

Gratitude: A Bloom in the Desert

Gratitude isn't just a fleeting feeling of thankfulness; it's a powerful practice that can significantly enhance our mental well-being. Taking time each day to appreciate the good things in your life, no matter how big or small, can shift your perspective and foster a sense of contentment.

Start a gratitude journal and write down a few things you're grateful for each day. Express appreciation to loved ones, savor a delicious meal, or take a moment to appreciate the beauty of nature. By weaving gratitude into the fabric of your daily life, you'll cultivate a more positive outlook and boost your overall well-being.

Seeing the World Anew: Engaging Your Senses

Mindfulness isn't just about internal experiences; it's also about connecting with the world around you. Engage your senses fully in everyday activities. Notice the vibrant colors of a sunset, savor the taste of your morning coffee, or feel the texture of the fabric against your skin. By paying close attention to these sensory details, you'll bring a richness and depth to your experience of the present moment.

Bringing Mindfulness to the Mundane: Everyday Practices

Mindfulness doesn't require long stretches of meditation or exotic retreats. The beauty lies in its simplicity and accessibility. Mindful eating is a powerful way to integrate mindfulness into your daily routine. Focus on the taste, texture, and aroma of your food, savoring each bite without distraction. Transform your commute into a mini-meditation by focusing on your breath and the sensations in your body. Even simple tasks like washing the dishes or folding laundry can become opportunities for mindfulness by focusing on the present moment movements and sensations.

Remember, cultivating mindfulness is a journey, not a destination. There will be days when your mind wanders, and that's perfectly okay. The key is to gently bring your attention back to the present moment without judgment. With consistent practice, mindfulness will become a natural part of your life, helping you experience greater joy, peace, and clarity in every moment.

CHAPTER 4

SETTING BOUNDARIES AND SAYING NO: PROTECTING YOUR SANCTUARY

Imagine your personal space as a tranquil garden. Lush greenery represents your energy, and vibrant flowers symbolize your well-being. But what happens when people constantly trample through your garden, demanding your time and attention? Boundaries are the invisible fences that protect your garden, ensuring your mental well-being doesn't get trampled underfoot.

The Fortress of Well-being: Why Boundaries Matter

Personal boundaries are the lines we draw between ourselves and others. They define what we consider acceptable behavior and how much of our time, energy, and resources we're willing to share. Healthy boundaries are essential for protecting our mental well-being. Without them, we become susceptible to burnout, resentment, and emotional manipulation.

Building the Fence: Communicating Boundaries Effectively

Setting boundaries isn't about being selfish; it's about self-care. The key lies in clear and assertive communication. Directly communicate your needs to others. For example, instead of saying, "I'm too busy" when someone asks you to work late, try, "I appreciate the offer, but I need to leave by 6 pm today to maintain a healthy work-life balance."

The Art of "No": A Powerful Tool

Learning to say "no" is a crucial aspect of setting boundaries. It empowers you to prioritize your well-being and avoid commitments that drain your energy. Remember, "no" is a complete sentence. You don't need to justify your refusal with elaborate explanations.

Prioritizing Self-Care: Defying Societal Pressures

Our society often glorifies busyness and overcommitment. Learning to say "no" and prioritize self-care can feel counterintuitive.   However, remember that a full cup overflows more readily than a depleted one. Taking time for activities that recharge you, whether it's reading a book, spending time in nature, or simply enjoying a quiet evening at home, isn't a luxury; it's a necessity for maintaining your mental well-being.

Boundaries are not about pushing people away; they're about creating healthy, respectful relationships. By communicating your needs clearly, learning to say "no" with confidence, and prioritizing self-care, you can create a safe space where your mental well-being can flourish. Remember, a well-tended garden is a haven for both yourself and those you choose to share it with.

CHAPTER 5

THE STRENGTH OF POSITIVE RELATIONSHIPS: WEAVING A SUPPORTIVE TAPESTRY

Life is a journey, and no one navigates it alone. Strong, positive relationships are the threads that weave a supportive tapestry around us. They provide a sense of belonging, love, and acceptance, acting as a buffer against life's challenges and fueling our mental well-being.

Investing in Connection: Nurturing Meaningful Bonds

Humans are social creatures wired for connection. Investing time and effort in nurturing meaningful relationships with loved ones is crucial for our mental health. This doesn't require grand gestures. Simple acts like sharing a meal with a friend, making a heartfelt phone call to a parent, or engaging in a meaningful conversation with your partner can significantly strengthen your bonds.

Building a Support System: A Safety Net for Life's

Challenges

Life throws curveballs. Having a robust support system in place helps navigate difficult times. These are the people you can confide in, who offer a listening ear and unwavering support during emotional storms. Build a support system that includes close friends, family members, a therapist, or a trusted confidant.

The Art of Communication: Speaking and Listening with Empathy

Healthy communication is the cornerstone of strong relationships. Learn to express your needs and feelings clearly and assertively. Actively listen to others, acknowledging their perspectives without judgment. Develop empathy, the ability to see the world through another's eyes, to foster understanding and deepen connections.

Boundaries: Protecting Your Well-being Within Relationships

Even the strongest relationships require boundaries. Communicate your needs clearly, whether it's needing time for yourself or establishing limits on what you're willing to tolerate. Healthy boundaries within relationships ensure you don't become emotionally drained or taken advantage of.

Positive relationships are a two-way street. By investing in them, nurturing communication, and setting boundaries, you create a supportive network that empowers you to face challenges with greater resilience and fosters a sense of well-being that enriches your life. Remember, the strength of the tapestry lies in the quality of the threads and how they're woven together.

CHAPTER 6

Taming the Inner Critic: Silencing the Voice of Doubt

We all have an inner critic – that nagging voice in our head that whispers doubts, judgments, and harsh self-criticism. While it may masquerade as a protector, this inner critic can become a relentless bully, chipping away at our self-esteem and hindering our mental well-being. The good news is that you can learn to tame this inner critic and transform its negativity into a force for growth.

Unmasking the Villain: Identifying Negative Self-Talk

The first step to silencing the inner critic is recognizing its patterns. Pay attention to your self-talk. What kinds of things do you say to yourself throughout the day? Is your inner voice predominantly critical, judgmental, and unforgiving? Common negative self-talk patterns include:

Personal attacks: Labeling yourself as "stupid," "incompetent," or "a failure."

Mind-reading: Assuming you know what others think about you, often in a negative light.

Fortune-telling: Predicting negative outcomes before they even happen.

Catastrophizing: Blowing minor setbacks out of proportion.

From Bully to Coach: Cultivating Self-Compassion

Once you identify your inner critic's tactics, it's time to challenge them. Instead of accepting its pronouncements as truth, practice self-compassion. Treat yourself with the same kindness and understanding you would offer a close friend struggling with similar challenges.

Would you call your friend a failure for making a mistake? No, you'd likely offer encouragement and support. Extend that same compassion to yourself. Remember, everyone makes mistakes. They're opportunities to learn and grow, not evidence of inadequacy.

Transforming Negativity: Reframing Self-Criticism

Instead of letting negative self-talk hold you back, use it as a springboard for growth. When the inner critic starts its tirade, reframe its message into something constructive.

For example, if you hear yourself say, "I'm such a bad public speaker," reframe it as, "Public speaking makes me nervous. I can practice more to feel more confident." This shift in focus empowers you to take action and improve, rather than dwelling on negativity.

Embracing Imperfection: The Beauty of Being Human

Society often bombards us with unrealistic expectations of perfection. This relentless pursuit of perfection fuels the inner critic and sets us up for disappointment. The truth is, imperfection is inherent to the human experience. We all make mistakes, stumble, and fall.

Accepting imperfection as part of your journey allows you to let go of self-criticism and embrace your authentic self. Focus on progress, not perfection. Celebrate your small victories, and learn from your setbacks.

33

Taming the inner critic is a continuous process. There will be days when its voice seems louder than ever. But with consistent effort and self-compassion, you can transform it from a source of negativity into a catalyst for growth and self-acceptance. Remember, you are worthy and deserving of love and respect, flaws and all.

CHAPTER 7

Managing Stress and Anxiety: Finding Calm in the Chaos

Stress and anxiety are unwelcome companions in today's fast-paced world. They can manifest as a knot of tension in your stomach, a racing heart, or a relentless stream of worry. Left unchecked, chronic stress and anxiety can take a toll on your mental and physical health. The good news is, there are effective strategies to manage these common struggles and cultivate inner peace.

The Body Remembers: Recognizing Signs and Symptoms

Stress and anxiety don't just manifest in your mind; they impact your entire being. Learn to recognize the physical, emotional, and behavioral signs that indicate you're under pressure. These can include:

Physical symptoms: Headaches, muscle tension, fatigue, changes in appetite or sleep patterns.

Emotional symptoms: Irritability, difficulty concentrating, feelings of overwhelm or worry.

Behavioral symptoms: Procrastination, social withdrawal, reliance on unhealthy coping mechanisms.

By tuning into these subtle cues, you can address stress and anxiety before they spiral out of control.

Lightening the Load: Practical Strategies for Reducing Stressors

Sometimes, the most effective way to manage stress is to reduce the source of the pressure. Identify the stressors in your life. Are you juggling too many commitments? Feeling overwhelmed at work? Can you delegate tasks, set boundaries, or prioritize your workload? Taking proactive steps to address the root causes of stress can significantly improve your well-being.

Finding Your Calm Center: Relaxation Techniques for Anxiety Relief

When stress and anxiety take hold, various relaxation techniques can help restore a sense of peace. Deep breathing exercises are a simple yet powerful tool. Focus on slow, controlled inhalations and exhalations, allowing your body to release tension with each exhale. Mindfulness practices like meditation can help quiet your mind and cultivate a sense of present-moment awareness.

Other techniques like progressive muscle relaxation or guided imagery can also be effective in promoting calmness and serenity.

Seeking Support: When Self-Help Strategies Fall Short

Sometimes, self-help strategies aren't enough. If chronic stress or anxiety significantly impacts your daily life, don't hesitate to seek professional support. Therapists can equip you with evidence-based tools to manage stress and anxiety, develop healthy coping mechanisms, and cultivate greater resilience.

There is no shame in seeking professional help. It's a sign of strength and self-care, demonstrating your commitment to reclaiming your mental well-being. Remember, you don't have to navigate stress and anxiety alone.

By recognizing the signs of stress and anxiety, implementing proactive strategies to reduce stressors, utilizing relaxation techniques, and seeking professional support when needed, you can cultivate a sense of calm and inner peace even amidst the chaos of daily life.

CHAPTER 8

EMBRACING A GROWTH MINDSET: BLOOMING WHERE YOU'RE PLANTED

Life is an unpredictable journey, filled with sunshine and stormy weather. It's inevitable that we'll encounter challenges and setbacks along the way. But how we respond to these experiences defines our mental well-being and shapes our future. This chapter delves into the power of cultivating a growth mindset, a perspective that views challenges as opportunities for learning and growth.

Beyond Obstacles: Building Resilience

Imagine a sunflower reaching towards the sun, its sturdy stalk bending but not breaking in the face of strong winds. This resilience is what we strive for – the ability to bounce back from setbacks and continue thriving. A growth mindset is the key to building this resilience.

People with a growth mindset believe that their abilities and intelligence are not fixed but can be developed through effort and learning. This empowers them to see challenges as opportunities to learn, grow, and become stronger.

Seeding Success: Learning from Setbacks

When faced with a setback, a fixed mindset might whisper, "I'm a failure," leading to discouragement and giving up. A growth mindset, however, embraces the setback as a learning experience. Ask yourself, "What can I learn from this? How can I do better next time?"

This shift in perspective transforms failures from roadblocks into stepping stones on your path to growth. Analyze your mistakes, identify areas for improvement, and develop strategies to overcome future hurdles.

Celebrating Milestones: Appreciating Progress

The path to growth is paved with small victories, not just monumental achievements. A growth mindset encourages you to celebrate these milestones, no matter how seemingly insignificant. Did you finally master that challenging yoga pose? Did you persevere through a difficult conversation? Acknowledge these victories, however small, as they represent progress on your journey.

Never Stop Blooming: Continuous Growth as a Way of Life

A growth mindset isn't about achieving perfection; it's about embracing the ongoing process of learning and improvement. There will always be new skills to acquire, new challenges to overcome, and new areas for self-discovery. Embrace this lifelong journey with curiosity and enthusiasm.

Commit to continuous learning, whether through reading self-help books, taking online courses, or simply stepping outside your comfort zone and trying new things. Remember, the most beautiful flowers bloom from the most resilient seeds.

Fostering a growth mindset, you equip yourself with the tools to navigate life's inevitable challenges with resilience. Setbacks become stepping stones, and failures transform into valuable lessons. Embrace the journey of continuous learning and growth, and watch yourself blossom into the best version of yourself.

CHAPTER 9

PRIORITIZING FUN AND PLAY: RECLAIMING THE JOY IN EVERYDAY LIFE

Remember the carefree days of childhood, filled with laughter, exploration, and the simple joy of play? Somewhere along the way, responsibilities and routines might have pushed those playful moments aside. But here's the secret: prioritizing fun and play isn't frivolous; it's essential for maintaining mental well-being. This chapter reignites the importance of incorporating leisure, laughter, and lightheartedness into your life.

Unearthing the Lost Treasure: Rediscovering Fun and Hobbies

Think back to activities you once enjoyed but haven't pursued in a while. Was it painting, playing music, dancing, or simply reading for pleasure? Reconnecting with these hobbies can reignite a sense of joy and fulfillment. Hobbies provide a creative outlet, a chance to explore new interests, and a sense of accomplishment as you develop your skills.

Laughter is the Best Medicine: Weaving Playfulness into Daily Life

Laughter isn't just a fleeting moment of amusement; it's a powerful tool for boosting mental well-being. Laughter reduces stress hormones, elevates mood, and strengthens social bonds. Make an effort to incorporate playful moments into your daily routine. Watch a funny movie with a friend, share a joke with a colleague, or simply find humor in the everyday.

The Magic of the Inner Child: Reconnecting with Your Playful Self

Remember the boundless curiosity and enthusiasm of your inner child? Reconnecting with this playful side can infuse your life with renewed vitality. Schedule time for activities that bring you pure joy, even if they seem childish to your adult mind. Go for a swing set ride, build a sandcastle at the beach, or engage in a playful board game night with loved ones.

Balancing Productivity with Play: A Recipe for Well-being

Prioritizing fun doesn't mean abandoning responsibilities. It's about achieving a healthy balance. Think of life as a delicious meal. Productivity is the nutritious main course, but without the occasional dessert – a playful activity, a moment of laughter – the meal becomes bland and unsatisfying.

Schedule dedicated time for work and chores, but also block out time for leisure activities. Remember, a well-rested and playful mind is a more productive mind in the long run.

Life shouldn't be an endless to-do list. By rediscovering the joy of play, incorporating laughter into your routines, and reconnecting with your inner child, you'll inject vibrancy and lightness into your days. Remember, a life infused with fun and play is a life filled with greater well-being, creativity, and resilience.

45

CHAPTER 10

Just as we seek medical attention for physical ailments, sometimes our mental health requires professional support. This chapter explores the importance of seeking help from a therapist or counselor, guiding you through the process and dispelling any stigma associated with mental health treatment.

Knowing When to Ask for Help: Recognizing the Need for Professional Intervention

Life's challenges can sometimes feel overwhelming. While self-help strategies and healthy lifestyle choices are crucial, there are times when professional intervention becomes necessary. Consider seeking help if:

Daily functioning is significantly impaired by stress, anxiety, or depression.

You're struggling to cope with difficult emotions or past

traumas.

You find yourself engaging in unhealthy coping mechanisms. Relationships are suffering due to unresolved emotional issues.

Remember, seeking professional help is a sign of strength and self-awareness. It demonstrates your commitment to improving your mental well-being and living a more fulfilling life.

Finding the Right Fit: Navigating the Search for a Therapist

The therapeutic relationship is key to successful treatment. Finding a therapist you feel comfortable and safe with is crucial. Ask friends or family for recommendations, or consult your doctor for referrals. Many therapists also have online profiles outlining their specialties and treatment approaches.

Understanding Your Options: A Glimpse into Different Therapies

There are various therapeutic modalities, each with its own approach to healing. Cognitive-behavioral therapy (CBT) focuses on identifying negative thought patterns and developing coping mechanisms. Psychodynamic therapy delves deeper into past experiences and their impact on present behavior. Explore different modalities and discuss your preferences with potential therapists to find the best fit for your needs.

Investing in Your Journey: Embracing Therapy as a Path to Wholeness

Therapy is a collaborative process that requires commitment from both you and the therapist. Be open and honest with your therapist, and actively participate in the sessions. Therapy is not a quick fix, but a journey towards healing and growth. Celebrate your progress, no matter how small, and trust the process.

Taking care of your mental health is just as important as taking care of your physical health. Seeking professional support doesn't diminish your strength; it empowers you to live a life filled with greater clarity, resilience, and emotional well-being. Remember, a therapist is a skilled guide on your journey towards a more fulfilling life.

CONCLUSION

Cultivating Inner Harmony - A Journey of Growth

As we reach the end of this journey together, we've explored a multitude of practices to cultivate mental well-being. From embracing mindfulness and setting boundaries to fostering positive relationships and prioritizing fun, you've gained valuable tools to navigate the complexities of life.

The Transformative Power Within:

Reflect on the transformative power these practices can have on your life. Imagine a life where you're not constantly on autopilot, but present in the moment, savoring the richness of each experience. Imagine healthy boundaries protecting your energy, allowing you to invest fully in the things that matter most. Imagine the strength and support offered by positive relationships, a safety net during challenging times.

Integrating the Tools:

The key to lasting change lies in integrating these practices into your daily routine. Start small. Dedicate a few minutes each day to mindfulness practice. Communicate your needs assertively when setting boundaries. Schedule time for activities that bring you joy. As these practices become ingrained in your daily life, they'll empower you to navigate challenges with greater resilience and cultivate a sense of inner peace.

A Journey, Not a Destination:

Remember, cultivating mental well-being is a journey, not a destination. There will be days when you stumble, when negativity creeps in, or when healthy habits fall by the wayside. That's perfectly okay. The important thing is to keep moving forward, to acknowledge your progress, and to recommit to your journey towards inner harmony.

Embrace the Journey, Embrace Yourself:

As you move forward, carry this affirmation with you: "I am

worthy of love, respect, and a life filled with well-being." Embrace the journey of self-discovery, celebrate your victories, and learn from your setbacks. With consistent effort and self-compassion, you can cultivate a sense of inner harmony and create a life that is both fulfilling and meaningful.

ABOUT THE AUTHOR

 Aria Vitality is a seasoned health professional known for her holistic approach to wellness. With years of experience in nutrition, fitness, and mindfulness, she empowers individuals to achieve optimal health through personalized strategies tailored to their unique needs. Aria's passion lies in promoting overall well-being, emphasizing the importance of balanced nutrition, regular physical activity, and mental resilience. Her dedication to fostering healthy lifestyles makes her a trusted guide in the journey towards vitality and longevity.

Indeed, Aria Vitality's expertise extends to the medical realm, as she holds a doctorate in a relevant field such as naturopathic medicine or integrative health. With her medical background, she brings a comprehensive understanding of the body's physiological processes and how they intersect with lifestyle choices. Aria's multidisciplinary approach integrates traditional medical knowledge with holistic practices, allowing her to address health concerns from a holistic perspective. Whether providing personalized consultations, conducting research, or educating communities, her medical training enriches her ability to empower individuals on their journey to optimal health and well-being.